BOOKS BY J.R. SOLONCHE

True Enough

POEMS

J.R. SOLONCHE

DOS MADRES

2019

DOS MADRES PRESS INC.
P.O.Box 294, Loveland, Ohio 45140
www.dosmadres.com   editor@dosmadres.com

Dos Madres is dedicated to the belief that the small press is essential to the vitality of contemporary literature as a carrier of the new voice, as well as the older, sometimes forgotten voices of the past. And in an ever more virtual world, to the creation of fine books pleasing to the eye and hand.

Dos Madres is named in honor of Vera Murphy and Libbie Hughes, the "Dos Madres" whose contributions have made this press possible.

Dos Madres Press, Inc. is an Ohio Not For Profit Corporation and a 501 (c) (3) qualified public charity. Contributions are tax deductible.

Executive Editor: Robert J. Murphy

Illustration & Book Design: Elizabeth H. Murphy
www.illusionstudios.net

Typeset in Adobe Garamond Pro & Footlight MT
ISBN 978-1-948017-47-3
Library of Congress Control Number: 2019944623

First Edition

ACKNOWLEDGEMENTS

The American Journal of Poetry
    "In the Park Next to the River"
    "That Red Wheelbarrow"

The Lake
    "Writing about Writing about Plum Blossoms While Ill by
        Ch'en Hsien-Change While Ill"

Offcourse: A Literary Journal
    "After Reading William Matthews and Then Alan Dugan"
    "Ashes to Ashes"
    "Awake from a Nap"
    "I Found a Pencil on the Road"
    "Sephora"

One Sentence Poems
    "The Pine Two-by-Four"

TABLE OF CONTENTS

True Enough

THE POEMS FINALLY EXPLAIN THEMSELVES

We are not polite.
We push through any crowd,
no matter how loud,
to get the light.
Furthermore, we are not proud.

FOR ALL AND FOR ONCE

It's all here.
The rain and the trees and the grass and the leaves falling
    and the leaves yet to fall and

the leaves already fallen.
It's all there.

The rain carries them down in its stainless steel arms onto
    the grass and onto the road.
It all fits together.

They know it all by heart.
The rain washes them for burial.

There is no need for measurements.
It cannot be otherwise.

Otherwise, because they multiply so quickly, the questions
    would be all there would be.
There is a law against the questions.

The questions are forbidden here and there.
The questions are permitted only in the dreams of the
    answers.

Then, like the rest of us, the questions are forgotten when
    the answers awaken.
The questions disappear in the light of day.

This is the wisdom of, "Here it is."
This is the wisdom of, "There you are."

SOMETIMES THE STORY IS SURREAL
AND SOMETIMES REAL, SIR

Sometimes the surface is the story.
Sometimes the story is the surface.
Sometimes you serve two mistresses.
Sometimes you miss the fair tresses.
Sometimes you miss the dark tresses.
Sometimes you mistreat both.
Sometimes you meet the fair.
Sometimes you meet the dark.
Sometimes they meet in the story.
Sometimes the story is the face only.
Sometimes the story is the eyes only.
Sometimes the story is the tear only.
Sometimes the story is the laugh only.
Sometimes the story is surreal and sometimes real, sir.

THE GEESE

I heard the *g'hank, g'hank, g'hank*
of the geese over the trees,
so I looked up to see them veer
in their vee over me, but I had
to look a second time to see
the last, way back behind, saying,
g'back, g'back, g'back.

THE VIRTUE IN VIRTUOSITY IS
THE VIRTUE OF THE CITY

The countryside does not make noise.
It lacks the lung power.

It lacks the voice.
The countryside does not draw attention to itself.

It lacks the fluorescent glow.
It lacks the neon glower.

The piano of the countryside is harder to play than the
     forte of the city.
The countryside sings solo.

The countryside sways slow.
The city has no soul,

but the city wants to be soulful,
so the city covers that hole with a lousy virtuoso hollow.

WHEN THE HONEYBEE

When the honeybee
flew from the flowering shrub

it had been hunting pollen on,
I swear I could see

a smile on the face
of the flowering shrub

in the place where a face
would be if it had one.

ON A WALK

On a walk with Jim and
his cousin Larry, Larry
said his dentist is also
his therapist. Or as he put
it, "My therapist is also my
dentist." "At the same time?"
I asked. "You would save
a lot of money if he were
your therapist and dentist at
the same time." "Yeah,"
he said. "But I see him much
more often as a therapist
than as a dentist." "So where
do you see him for sessions?"
I said. "In his dentist's office?
In the chair? With the big light
in your face? You should.
It's the perfect place to talk
about your childhood traumas
and your mother and your father
and all that stuff. And he could
put you under the gas to get
the truth out of you." At this point,
Larry walked away to talk to Jim.
I hope his therapist is a good dentist.

AFTER READING WILLIAM MATTHEWS
AND THEN ALAN DUGAN

My eyes burn.
My mouth is numb.
My fingers drum the desk.
My dumbness is dumbstruck.
My lips open like wood:
You will never be this good.
The words fall on the desk.
I pick them up and put them back.
My lips open like wood:
You will never be this good.
I leave my words and go away.
They'll evaporate in about a day.

AT THE CONSTRUCTION SITE

Although the construction
is done at the construction

site, they left the big
Caterpillar backhoe

asleep on its haunches,
a yellow guard dog from hell.

AUTUMN

Master of mixed messaging,
Groucho of the seasons,
it sings, "Hello, I must be going!"
as I walk from home to wetland
to cornfield to houses to retired
farmer's retired farm, each stretch
of shade another welcome mat
of winter, while summer, through
gaps between the ambivalent trees,
flips me its shorter and shorter
middle finger of sun.

AWAKE FROM A NAP

Awake from a nap in the back,
I blink.

I see the sun hanging upside down from the clouds.
I blink.

I see a goldfinch hanging upside down from the birdfeeder.
I blink

I see a foolish old poet hanging upside down from the
world.
I blink.

I blink.
I blink.

CONGENIALLY CONGENITAL CONJUNCTION

Let us place our bodies together, genitals to genitals.
Let us be friendly and amiable.

Let us do this freely, freely without pressure,
free of obligation, guilt-free, of freedom free, sure to be unsure.

Let us put our bodies close, closer than close,
the closest two bodies can be.

Let them be the most bodies, therefore the least souls.
Let our bodies be all bodies that say, "What are souls?"

Let us put our bodies so close there shall be no space for souls.
Let our souls wander space.

Let our souls leave our bodies and leave our bodies alone.
Bodies are best when left to their own devices.

That's how they devised it.
Let our souls fend for themselves.

Let them find another home away from home.
It will be their loss, poor lost souls.

STUDENT AND ZEN MASTER

"Master, will I ever become Enlightened?"
asked the student.

"Yes, as long as you don't put your mind to it,"
laughed the Master.

THE LAST EPIPHANY

Go out and have an epiphany about yourself,
she said. Everyone, sooner or later,
has an epiphany which changes his life.
The problem is, I've already experienced
too many epiphanies about myself.
I'm over-epiphanied. I'm all epiphanied out.
One more epiphany about myself,
and I'll crack. No thanks.
I'll change my life by getting older.

FATE IS FATE REGARDLESS
OF WHERE YOU SIT

I hear the acorns
falling. If Newton's
tree had been an oak,
one of these would be
as famous as an apple.
Their tough luck.

FOUR PURPLE CONE FLOWERS

Not exactly purple,
not quite cones,

the tallest in the garden,
the most erect,

they look like
they are on horseback.

Tight as a string quartet.
Close as a barbershop quartet.

I think they are unkillable.
The rainstorms have not killed them.

The wind storms have not killed them.
The first frost will not kill them.

Yes, yes, I know they will die,
all together, at once, in their time,

but I will refuse to say *killed,*
I will never say *killed.*

BOOK GHAZAL

Remember Jimmy Walker, the mayor of New York?
He said that no one ever died from reading a book.

He was undoubtedly right, but I wonder
how many suicides got their idea from reading a book.

If I were stranded on a desert island with only one,
the *Complete Works of Shakespeare* would be my book.

Of all the hundreds of poems of Emily Dickinson,
only six are about reading books.

The best memory I have as a kid going to school
is cracking the spine, then inhaling the smell of a brand
  new book.

One of the eight Chinese common emblems,
the symbol of the power to ward off evil spirits, is a book.

  So, Solonche, what do you think of this poem
   you've written?
  I think it would be a damn shame if it doesn't see
   the inside of a book.

GOING OUTSIDE TO LOOK AT THE SKY
AFTER FAILING TO PERSUADE MY WIFE
TO MAKE LOVE

There is nothing like the night sky
to clear your head and your heart,
especially one such as this January
night sky with its myriad stars,
brilliant as chrome and its moon,
full to overflowing with icy whiteness.
There is nothing like it to put you
in your place.
          So sleep,
sleep and dream, as you sometimes do,
that dream about us, that dream
that makes me jealous of myself
when you tell me about it in the morning.
I am not angry anymore. I am only
disappointed, only a little disappointed,
as I have always been, about everything,
since first I knew what imagination was.
And desire.

GRATITUDE

Now I want
to thank *now*
for getting me
started, without
which this page
would be as blank
as my stare was
a moment ago,
and thank as well
ago for ending.
No, *ending.*
No, *no.*

HELGA

She should never
have agreed
to appear in that film
about him,
that fat old woman
in that ridiculous hat.
At least he was dead by then.

I ASKED THE FAMOUS NOVELIST

I asked the famous novelist
if he wrote poetry. "No," he said.
"I'll leave that to you." I nodded
and smiled, but there was something
in his tone I didn't like.
Or the way he held his head.

I FOUND A PENCIL ON THE ROAD

I found a pencil on the road.
It looked like it had been whittled
to expose the lead, not sharpened
with a sharpener. Used for about
two inches of writing. What? Math
homework? Doodles? Poems?
The eraser was rubbed down to gone,
so it must have been poems. I took
it home, wrote this with it, broke it
in half, and threw it out.

I MET SISTER DEER

I met Sister Deer.
"Because you are a living thing,
I know that you suffer,
so how can you be sober?"
I asked. "We Deer do not suffer
the way you Humans do.
We do not count the days
to death the way you do,"
she said, trotting away.
I met Brother Frog.
"Because you are a living thing,
I know that you suffer,
so how can you be sober?"
I asked. "We Frogs do not suffer
the way you Humans do.
We do not count the days
to death the way you do,"
he said, hopping away.
I met Sister Rabbit.
"Because you are a living thing,
I know that you suffer,
so how can you be sober?"
I asked. "We Rabbits do not suffer
the way you Humans do.

We do not count the days
to death the way you do,"
she said, bounding away.
I met Brother Snake.
"Because you are a living thing,
I know you that you suffer,
so how can you be sober?"
I asked. "We Snakes do not suffer
the way you Humans do.
We do not count the days
to death the way you do,"
he said, slithering away.
I met Sister Skunk.
"Because you are a living thing,
I know that you suffer,
so how can you be sober?"
I asked. "We Skunks do not suffer
the way you Humans do.
We do not count the days
to death the way you do,"
she said, sashaying away.
I met Brother and Sister Owl.
"Because you are living things,
I know that you suffer,
so how can you be sober?"

I asked. "We Owls do not suffer
the way you Humans do.
We do not count the days to death
the way you do," they said,
going back to speak Owl
from the woods to the woods.

I OFTEN WONDER WHAT IT WILL BE LIKE

I often wonder what it would be like,
the morning I do not wake up.
I wonder if it will be like this winter
morning, for instance, the sun shining
brightly enough but cold and distant,
the lake frozen and silent, a desert of ice,
overhead a v of geese practicing
to stay in shape while another v
follows behind like the other half of
a w hurrying to catch up, my neighbor
in a bathrobe going out to the end of
the driveway to get the Sunday paper.
I hope it is but if not, I will understand.
I hope the news is better but if not,
I will understand.

I WANTED TO PICK IT

I wanted to pick it,
a mercy killing,
the solitary blue
cornflower, as far as
I could see, the only
one as far as I could
see, but, no, I walked
on, hoping no one else
would come along
to see it after me,
unless he, too, were
a poet, for a poet
would be the only one
permitted to pick
the last blue cornflower
as far as we could see.

I WENT TO GET NEW TIRES

I went to get new tires.
Sitting in the waiting area,
I heard the boss sneeze
from his desk in the corner.
"Bless you," I said. He
didn't say thank you.
I guess he didn't hear me.
A few minutes later,
he sneezed again. "Bless
you," I said again, louder.
Again he didn't say thank you.
He must have heard me,
so why didn't he thank me?
Is he simply impolite?
Is he an atheist and doesn't
believe in blessings? Is
he a fucking anti-Semite
and won't be blessed by a Jew?
I hoped to hear a third sneeze,
so I could say, "Bless you"
one more time, but sad
to say, he didn't sneeze again.
I left it a mystery. Too bad.
I was itching for a fight.

IMPROVISATION ON A LINE
OF WALLACE STEVENS

The fault lies with an over-human god.
Too familiar therefore contemptible,
he makes us break the mirror of himself.
He speaks in the dark accents of our tribe
and in the numbers of our victories.
His iron words were forged in our fires.
Nothing was alien to us except
the law that we learned by heart in one
generation. He was a holy man
with no desert, a dreamer with no sleep.
He was lonelier than the leper is.
We took him in. What did we want of him?
We wanted him to be our opposite,
our window to a better world than ours,
not a mirror. We used our shields for that.

IN TERMS OF THOUGHT

Here I am,
on thought's terms.

IN THE PARK NEXT TO THE RIVER

All the butterflies were white.
Then there was a yellow butterfly.

Some of the flowers were yellow.
Some of the flowers were blue.

Some of the flowers were white.
None of the flowers were red.

A sailboat welcomed the wind with open arms.
The wind was white in the sail.

A woman who was tall walked two dogs.
One dog was black.

One dog was white.
A woman who was short walked one dog.

The dog was black and white.
I forgot my guide to the flowers.

I forgot my guide to the butterflies.
I forgot my guide to the sailboats.

I forgot my guide to the wind.
I forgot my guide to the dogs.

I forgot my guide to the women.
I forgot my guide to open arms.

IT MAKES NO DIFFERENCE WHEN IT WAS BECAUSE IT IS ONLY A PRONOUN NOW

It was either before I was Younger
Or it was after I was Younger.

It was either before I was Older
Or it was after I was Older.

It was either before the Moon
Or it was after the Moon.

It was either before the dream of the Song
Or it was after the dream of the Song.

It was either before the First Time
Or it was after the First Time.

It was either before the blossoms of the Wild Cherry
Or it was after the blossoms of the Wild Cherry.

It was either before the orange cat ran Away
Or it was after the orange cat ran Away.

It was either before the lake froze Over
Or it was after the lake froze Over.

It was either before the geese Returned
Or it was after the geese Returned.

It was either before the Thunderstorm
Or it was after the Thunderstorm.

It was either before the neighbor Died
Or it was after the neighbor Died.

It was either before the Vodka
Or it was after the Vodka.

It was either before I knew the Answer
Or it was after I knew the Answer.

It was either before I could Remember
Or it was after I could Remember.

It was either before I found the word for It
Or it was after I found the word for It.

It was either before Then
Or it was after Then.

JUST MY LUCK AND NOBODY ELSE'S

It was at the Square.
She found the White Rose on the desk.

She looked left.
It was the White Rose I left there.

She looked right.
"What's that?" he asked.

This was later.
 "A white rose," she said.

This was in the elevator.
She smiled.

It was in her hand.
"What for?" he said.

"For luck," she said.
She smiled.

It was in her hand.
Then the White Rose went down.

And she went down with the White Rose.
It was in her hand.

And the years went down.
They were in her hands.

The years went down, went down, went down.
All the years went down with the last White Rose in the World.

It was in her hand.
They were in her hands, in her hands, in her hands.

One white rose filled up with all of the years in the world
    went down.
It was just my luck and nobody else's.

LAST PEONY

I couldn't resist picking it,
as I could not resist picking the first.
Bringing it in, putting it in a vase,
like fitting a new candle to a holder.
The last peony in the garden,
round, pink on pink on pink, still
opening one upon the other,
among a dozen spent peonies,
each as dark as a burnt match head
the wind has blown out
before the summer can catch.

LIFE CAN TAKE YOU ONLY SO FAR

After that you're on your own.
The movie was boring.

It was too true to life.
"How tall are you?" he asked.

"Why do you ask?" she asked.
He asked because he needed to know.

He needed to know because he asked.
"Five-eleven," she said.

"I'm five-eleven and a half," he said.
It was too true to life.

It was too false to life.
It was too much life.

It was too little life.
The movie was boring.

He left before the end.
That was the end.

He was on his own.

Life can take you only so far.

LUCK

A black cat crossed
my path today,
and then crossed it
back the other way.
Was the bad luck
taken back again?
So far so good.

MILK SNAKE

The baby
      milk snake
            crossed
            my path
    as long
as this way
      but black
            and orange
      instead
            of black
    and
white.

MY NEIGHBOR'S BODY

I don't believe a body has a soul,
but I do believe a soul has a body.

I saw the body on the floor where he left it.
I heard the soul crying from the cat on the bed
    where he left it.

ODDLY, IN TIME, WITH NO OPPOSITION TO OPPOSITES, IT ALL EVENS OUT

The days do not know how.

They stand by and let the years do the heavy work.

This is because the years are so good at it.

They have had so much practice.

It is second nature to them.

The days admire the handiwork of the years.

The days marvel at their strength.

The days wonder at their skill.

 "Someday we will do that," say the days.

And, though no one will believe it, they do.

ON THE BRIDGE ABOVE THE RIVER

On the bridge above the river, I had four souls.
They followed the river from north to south.

My first soul was blue, blue from the blue of the sky to
 the north.
My second soul was green, green from the green of the
 trees along the riverbank.

My third soul was black, black from the shadow of the
 bridge on the river.
My fourth soul was silver, silver from the sun reflected on
 the river to the south.

I had four souls today, one more soul than the river.
It had the blue soul, the green soul, the silver soul, but
 not the black soul.

When I left the bridge, I left three souls with the river.
Only the black soul of the shadow of the bridge did I
 keep for myself.

I keep it close to this day.
It is the only one I have.

OUT OF MIND OUT OF SIGHT

I was out of sight.
I used up all my sight seeing you.

(If this were a love poem, I could say that.
I could sing that so convincingly you would believe it.
This is not a love poem, so I cannot say that.)

I was out of mind.
I used up all my mind thinking of you.

(If this were a love poem, I could say that.
I could sing that so convincingly you would believe it.
This is not a love poem, so I cannot say that.)

I am blind.
This is a love poem, so it is true.

I am thoughtless.
This is a love poem, so it is true.

OUT OF MIND, OUT OF SIGHT

Once there was a Thought.
It was a speck of Light.
It was one twinkle of a distant Star.
It could have been a Photon.
It came to me in the dark from the Dark.
But it was never Born.
It left in the Dark.
But it never Died.
It was not in mind until it was in Sight.
But it was never in Mind.
It was not a Surprise.
But it was always out of Sight.
Once there was a Thought.
It fit me to a tee, Though.

OWLS

Dusk and my neighbor's telephone has stopped ringing.
The loudest sound is the owl pair talking,

the hissy tenor whisper of the male
in the woods on one side of the road,

and the hissy contralto whisper of the female
in the woods on the other side of the road,

and the silences long in between the loud whispering
as the clock of the world slows down to owl time.

I PITY THE HONEY BEE

I pity the honey bee
that has sought out,
this chilly October
afternoon, the last
of the pink impatiens,
but I envy the flower
it has sought and found.

PROPHECY

It could have been any way.

It could have been one way or another.

It was decided, but no decision was made.

There was a conclusion, but it was not concluded.

No one had a clue until it was done.

Then the dots were unconnected.

No one laughed, but there was laughter.

Then the father left the son.

Then the mother left the daughter.

Then the husband left the wife.

Then the wife left the husband.

Then the queen picked up the silver knife.

Then she blessed the martyred hosts.

Then she hailed the dominion of the galaxy of ghosts.

SEPHORA

Did Moses' Midianite wife,
Zipporah, really use all this perfume,

all this lipstick,
all this eye shadow,

all this eye liner,
all this lash lengthener,

all this body lotion,
all this face powder,

so much all this that
if I weren't already seventy-two

and thereby have no reason to,
I swear I'd swear off sex?

THAT RED WHEELBARROW

How disappointed I was
when I found out
that the story wasn't true,
that he had noticed it
through the window
of the room of the sick
little girl he was called
to tend to, but that it
actually belonged
to an old black street
vendor in Rutherford.
Of course, so much did
depend on it regardless
of whose it was,
and the rain water
did still glisten on it,
and the white chickens
were still white and
were still going to get
their throats cut. So
perhaps it's a good thing
it was the street vendor's.
The little girl would
have given them names.

THERE WAS THAT, THERE WAS WAS,
   ## THERE WAS THERE

The lake was there as it always is.
And the reflections of the clouds were there
as they always are when there are clouds.
And the sun was there, the only late comer, for the clouds
had blocked its way there.
And the great blue heron was still there until it was not.
And I was there, which should go without saying, but cannot.

THE BEAUTIFUL BARMAID

The beautiful
barmaid
has made

me mad,
for she moves
gorgeous-

ly in her
pants and
suspenders

like a tigress,
like a lioness,
like a panther.

THE BEAUTIFUL WOMAN

The beautiful woman
had an accent. "What
part of the UK are you from?"
I asked. "Southeast London,"
she said. "Please do something
for me," I said. "Could
you say *Darling*? And could
you sound like you mean it?
You can look at your husband
while saying it," I said. So she
turned to look at her husband
and said, "Darling." But it
didn't sound like she meant it.
That was fine with me. It was
still the best *Darling* I've ever heard.

THE BIRD

The bird
in the beech tree

can count to 2 –
Whit who –

and 3 –
Whit who whee –

but not to 1
apparently.

THE CHILDREN

are playing in the schoolyard.
Some are running.

Some are skipping.
Some are swinging.

Some are kicking a ball.
Some are tossing a disk.

Two are flying.
I am a child.

I am not running.
I am not skipping.

I am not swinging.
I am not kicking a ball.

I am not tossing a disk.
I am flying, flying, flying.

THE CLOUDS

The clouds look like clouds.
This is not their fault.

And when they look like my mind,
that, too, is not their fault.

THE DARK CLOUDS SO

The dark clouds so
flow over the sky
to over-flowing
that when I heard
the siren of the fire
truck heading east,
I thought the firemen
were responding to
tomorrow burning.

THE DAY IS THE NIGHT

The day is the night
with light

but with less
on its mind.

THE LAKE IN THE RAIN

The lake in the rain
remembers when
it was the rain
and quietly cries
in the depth of its sleep,
which, if you carefully listen,
sounds like rain on a lake.

THE LAKE IS A GOOD LISTENER

The lake is a good listener.
It has an open mind.
It listens to the wind without turning away.
It listens to the trees without yawning.
It listens to the frogs without laughing in their faces.
It listens to the geese without mimicking them.
It even listens to me, I, who have so much less to say
than the geese, than the frogs, than the trees, than the wind,
without shaking its head and mumbling under its breath.

THE MOST BEAUTIFUL BEAUTY

The most beautiful woman I ever saw
had no face.
And that was as it should be they said,
they all said.

The most beautiful symphony I ever heard
made no sound.
And that was as it should be they said,
they all said.

The most beautiful flower I ever beheld
had no color.
And that was as it should be they said,
they all said.

The most beautiful building I ever went in
held no roof.
And that was as it should be they said,
they all said.

The most beautiful poem I ever read
spoke no word.
And that was as it should be, they said,
they all said.

THE PASTURE COVERED IN FROST

The pasture covered in frost
this morning is missing
only the old horse waiting
absolutely still by the fence,
the only movement the slow
rising of the steam of his breath.

THE PINE TWO-BY-FOUR

The pine two-by-four,
now newly sawn
exactly by the carpenter,
smells exactly like a newborn.

THE PURPLE CHRYSANTHEMUM

The purple chrysanthemum
is halfway dead,

its brown, dead half
imparting its living purple

half with a desperate
liveliness wholly its own.

THE SHADOW OF THE FLAG

The shadow of the flag
on my neighbor's lawn
flies in the sky of the wall
of his house. Surely it is an omen,
more so since the flag is not upside down.

THE THREE-MONTH OLD

The three-month old
in the stroller was staring at me.
What was she thinking?
I tell you honestly,
I would pay her college tuition
to know what was in her three-month old
mind while she was staring at me.

TO THE EDITOR WHO SAID
HE COULD NOT PUBLISH MY POEM
UNTIL HE KNEW WHAT IT MEANT

So publish some other one,
one that you know what it means.
How about this one?

TODAY THE FIRST

Today the first
yellow leaves of fall
fell. I picked them up
from the ground and
threw them back up
into the tree. "Here,"
I said. "Take these back.
It's too soon. Stop."
"Okay," the tree said
and stopped.

TWO KOANS FOLLOWED BY FREE ASSOCIATION

When you can do nothing, what can you do?
What is the color of the wind?

What is the color of nothing?

When you can do nothing, what color are you?

When the wind is doing nothing, is it still the wind?

When the mind is doing nothing, is it still the mind?

When the mind wants to do nothing, is it doing nothing?

Or is it doing something called *wants to do nothing?*

Is the mind the wind on its feet?

Is the wind the mind on its back?

What is the color of your mind?

What color can the wind make?

When you can, what can you?

When you can't, what can't you?

WALKING HOME

Walking home,
I followed the sky
to the window
of my neighbor's
house, where,
because of the wall's
angle, it was, briefly,
the house of the sky.

WHAT I LEARNED TODAY

I did not know
that hummingbirds
make sounds
other than humming
until just now when
I heard one chirping
like any ordinary bird
while humming.

WHEN THE POET SAID

When the poet said
there's no such thing
as an ugly tree, he lied.
I saw two today

WHENEVER I HEAR

Whenever I hear
the big sound
of the big-ass woodpecker
pounding on the big ash tree,
I smile in approval appropriately.

WRITING ABOUT
WRITING ABOUT PLUM BLOSSOMS WHILE ILL
BY CH'EN HSIEN-CHANG
WHILE ILL

I am not ill, but if I were ill,
I would be lying in bed.
A pot of green tea on the bed table.

I would read "Writing About
Plum Blossoms While Ill"
by the philosopher Ch'en Hsien-chang.

A sentence. Then hang
my head a little to the side.
Then a sip of green tea.

Then look out the window.
Then close my eyes. Nod.
Then slowly swallow.

Read another sentence. Lift my head
a little. A sip of green tea.
Look at the invisible plum tree.

WILD CHERRY IN MID-APRIL

White-haired
old man,

white-whiskered
old poet,

pausing on
his journey

in front
of my house,

leaning on
his staff,

laughing in
the rain at us.

WITH NOT A CLOUD ALL DAY

With not a cloud all day
to contest it, the sun
had the sky to itself
until a crow looked, then
came to cast the scowl
of itself across the blue.

YOUR QUESTION

Ask the wind bending the trees your question.

You will get an answer.

It will be the wind's answer.

Ask the trees bending in the wind your question.

You will get an answer.

It will be the trees' answer.

For the truth, ask your question of both the wind and the trees.

4:44 IN THE AFTERNOON

It is quiet.

It is quiet outside.

It is quiet on the road.

It is dark and quiet on the road

If I were a child, you would say, "What an amazing poem!"

If I were a child, you would say, "What a precocious child!"

If I were a child, you would say, "You will be a famous poet
    someday!"

If I were a child you would say, "Exclamation point!"

I am looking forward to my second childhood.

If I were a child.

If only I were a child.

ASHES TO ASHES

Jim's brother died last week. We went
to the funeral home to pick up the ashes.
"Why is it called a funeral home?" I said.
"Is it the home of fuckin funerals?"
"Could be. Maybe because it's more
like our home away from home," Jim said.
"It's heavy," said the funeral director
handing Jim a shopping bag with the box
with the ashes with his brother without a home.
"He ain't heavy," Jim said. "He's my brother."
The funeral director didn't laugh. "Animals
don't go to funeral homes when they die,"
I said. "Shit, why do we?" "Right," Jim said.
"The whole fuckin earth is their home."
"So what are you going to do with Mike's ashes?"
I said. "Spill them somewhere nice," Jim said.
"Around here? I thought he didn't come from
around here," I said. "Maybe I should send
it up to his wife in New Hampshire. She
ought to decide what to do," Jim said.
"I guess so," I said. "But you have the ashes.
Don't you think you ought to decide what
to do with them?" "Maybe. After all, I did
know him longer than his wife did," Jim said.

"Let's go find some place nice." "That place on the Delaware?" I said. "Yeah," Jim said. "Where we saw the three girls in the raft take off their tops and wave at us?" I said. "Yeah, that's the one," Jim said. "That place."

WHEN I SAW THE HAWK CIRCLING WIDE

When I saw the hawk circling wide
while whistling,
then stalling directly above
my head to show me how
its underside had turned into sunlight,
for the first time I knew what
I really wanted a poem to do, to circle wide,
whistle, then stall directly above
your head to show how its underside
turns into sunlight.

I WENT TO THE LIBRARY

I went to the library
to give my two new books
to Matt, the head librarian,
to put on the shelf. "Hey,
Matt," I said. "Here are my
latest books to put on the poetry
shelf." (It's a small library.
It has only one poetry shelf.)
"Well, you know, I have
to review them," he said.
"Okay," I said. "You have
three of my books already,
so just read them and put
them on the shelf next to
those." "Well," he said,
"there's very little space."
(Matt says "well" a lot.)
"Okay," I said. "But, you
know, they're really thin
books. They're poetry. Like
the other three. Just squeeze
them in, okay?" (I say "okay"
a lot.) I think he smiled. "I'll
review them," he said. "Oh,

one more thing," I said. "You
spelled my name wrong."
I handed him the page in
the catalogue I printed out
for one of my books. Next
to author was "Salanche, J.R."
"Oh, yeah, I see," Matt said.
"That's tough. I'll have to delete
the whole thing and enter it
from scratch all over again."
He shook his head. I think
he smiled again. Or he could
have been smiling the whole
time. "Okay," I said. "Thanks."
So much for immortality.

I DO NOT WANT TO WRITE

a poem about the deer
tracks in the snow,
but it is getting harder
and harder to find things
I do not not want to write about.

EXCUSE

I wanted to tell the truth,
but you see,

the truth had better things to do
and wouldn't let me.

A POET SENT ME HIS BOOK

A poet sent me his book.
The cover is beautiful.

The poems are not so beautiful.
Of course, it's possible

the poet did not intend them to be.
But the cover is so beautiful

I ripped it off, carefully, carefully,
and framed it to hang on the wall.

SO MUCH FOR SO MUCH SO

What happened to the sun?
I will drink my coffee with my eyes closed.

I will stay indoors until the sun comes out and says,
    "Come out!"
I will not shoo the squirrels from the feeder filled with
    black oil seeds.

They do not care what happened to the sun.
Neither do the black capped chickadees.

Let them who can fend for themselves do so.
I can fend for myself.

But I cannot fend off myself.
What happened to the sun?

They're lined up waiting for weed in Massachusetts.
A judge has told the so-called president to go to hell.

Say what you will, but I will not defend myself.
What happened to the sun?

The sun has set in the west.
The sun has set in California.

The sun has set California on fire.
A judge has told California to go to hell.

What happened to the sun?
Sol Invictus, must we pray in Latin for you to hear us?

Sol Invictus, for what must we pray?
There aren't enough prayers to go around.

There are too many poems to go around.
There are too many poems in the world.

The world does not need so many poems.
Let us trade poems for prayers.

Let us turn in one-hundred poems in exchange for one prayer.
That is a fair exchange.

I will begin.
I will give up one hundred poems for one prayer.

Sol Invictus, save us!
Sol Invictus, pro nobis, ut Deus!

WHO HAS KISSED

Who has kissed
the night on the mouth,

the night on the mouth,
the night on the mouth,

to leave this lipstick
stain of full moon,

stain of full moon,
stain of full moon?

THE OLD WEEPING WILLOW TREE

At the edge of the swamp,
the old weeping willow tree,
near death, all dried up, all cried out
from weeping out of pity for the world,
has but one green tear left for self-pity.

ANOTHER EXCUSE

If I did not take your words to heart,
it is only because
my heart took me to your words.

AN ANGEL

I met an angel.
She had the blondest of blonde hair.

She had the clearest of clear skin.
She had the bluest of blue eyes.

She had the lithest of lithe limbs.
She had the softest of soft speech.

I walked around her to see if she had wings.
I did this slyly, pretending to be doing something else.

She did not have wings.
But she was an angel.

Of that I am positive.
I said something.

I do not remember what I said.
It was harmless.

It was friendly.
It was not foolish.

She was not embarrassed.

"I'm from Minnesota," she said. "Minnesota is a good state."

"Yes, I know," I said. "Minnesota is the second best state
    in America.
That's in a recent survey by Newsweek Magazine."

That's not what I wanted to say.
I wanted to say, "Minnesota must be Heaven.

Did you leave your wings at home?"
This is how to speak to an angel.

This is how to remember an angel.
This is how to write a poem about an angel.

This is how to be gracious to an angel.
This is how to be graceful about being old.

This is how to not be grateful for being old.
This is how to regret being old one more time.

This is how to write a poem about being old.
This about how to hold the poem in until it grows wings.

This is how to hide the poem under your hat.

This is how to do it until you meet an angel from Minnesota.

JIM AND I WENT TO VISIT

Jim and I went to visit
a colleague in the nursing
home. "He's in good spirits,"
I said as we were leaving.
"Yeah," said Jim, "but I would
rather the good spirits be in me."

KOOSER

Ted, you say your
poem about your dead
parents is dark. I say
you do darkness with
a light touch, so the rest
of us may see better in it.

ABOUT THE WHITE WHALE

About the white whale
they are all wrong.
It is the blank paper on
the desk that he pursues
with the harpoon of his pen
and nothing more.

THE PHILOSOPHY OF CONSOLATION

I have never read words that have ever consoled me.
It was always the wings of the music through the windows.

It was always the wings of the wind on the hills.
It was always the wings of the sun on the hawks.

It was always the wings of the clouds over the lakes.
I have never heard words that have ever consoled me.

It was always the language of the wings.
It was always the voice of the wings.

It was always the sound of the wings.
It was always the whisper of the wings.

It was always the wings that consoled me.
It was always the wings.

MY NEIGHBOR HAS

My neighbor has
a fake wishing well
in his yard. It must be
for making fake wishes.
It's old and decrepit.
It's an eyesore. I wish
it would disappear.

ONE OF THE BIRCH TREES

One of the birch trees
at the point is angled so
steeply, so extended out
over the water, it looks
like a fisherman has planted
it that way and left, the lure
long gone to the bottom, the line
long unspooled, unlooped, and blown away in the breeze.

THE SWANS

The swans on the lake want
to have nothing to do with the geese,

so they keep their distance,
fortunate to have all that distance to keep.

AFTER THE READING

After the reading,
there were questions
as there always are,
but this one I never
heard before. "How do
you decide what becomes
a poem and what doesn't?"
"Well, I don't decide.
The poem decides when
it wants to become itself,
so it's really out of my
hands," I said and went
to the bar for another drink.

YOU WEREN'T THERE WHEN I WAS THERE

I wasn't there when you were there.
We missed each other.

Life was like that.
Life was missing each other.

Life was missing.
Time was there.

Space was there.
Silence was there in abundance.

The least of life was there.
Thousands of breaths beat in our chests.

Thousands of heartbeats breathed in our lungs.
Life was missing.

Others were there when you were there without me.
Others were there when I was there without you.

When you were there, I was elsewhere.
When I was there, you were elsewhere.

That elsewhere may just as well have been nowhere.
That other elsewhere may just as well have been another nowhere.

We were nowhere to be found.
Life was missing.

A COLLEAGUE AND I WERE TALKING

A colleague and I were talking
in the hall between classes. "I just
read that most men think about sex
more than anything else," she said.
"I guess I'm not most men because
I don't think about sex more than
anything else," I said. "No?" she said.
"No," I said. "Well, what do you think
about more than anything else?" she said.
"I think about poetry more than anything
else," I said. "Oh," she said. "I get it.
You think about something you can actually
do something about." "That's right," I said.
"You know, that's right," I said again.

ABOUT THE AUTHOR

J.R. SOLONCHE is the author of *Beautiful Day* (Deerbrook Editions), *Won't Be Long* (Deerbrook Editions), *Heart's Content* (Five Oaks Press), *Invisible* (nominated for the Pulitzer Prize by Five Oaks Press), *The Black Birch* (Kelsay Books), *I, Emily Dickinson & Other Found Poems* (Deerbrook Editions), *In Short Order* (Kelsay Books), *Tomorrow, Today & Yesterday* (Deerbrook Editions), *If You Should See Me Walking on the Road* (Kelsay Books), *The Time of Your Life* (forthcoming April 2020 from Adelaide Books), *The Porch Poems* (forthcoming 2020 from Deerbrook Editions), and coauthor of *Peach Girl: Poems for a Chinese Daughter* (Grayson Books). He lives in the Hudson Valley.

For the full Dos Madres Press catalog:
www.dosmadres.com